MICHAEL PALMER

BLAKE'S NEWTON

BLAKE'S NEWTON
by
MICHAEL PALMER

Illustrations by Bobbie Creeley

BLACK SPARROW PRESS · LOS ANGELES · 1972

Some of these poems originally appeared in:
*Joglars, Friendly Local Press, Sumac, Gros-
seteste Review, Caterpillar, Spectrum,*
and *Open Reading.*

Prose 12 was first published by the Barn
Dream Press in the pamphlet, *Plan of the
City of O.*

Black Sparrow Press
P. O. Box 25603
Los Angeles, California 90025

LIBRARY OF CONGRESS CATALOGING IN PUBLICATION DATA

Palmer, Michael, 1943-
  Blake's Newton.

  Poems.
  I. Title.
  PS3566.A54B5   811'.5'4   72-6943
  ISBN 0-87685-129-4
  ISBN 0-87685-128-6 (pbk.)

CONTENTS

—1—

Blake's Newton

ITS FORM

Its form, at tables by fours
leap . . . relieved of their weight.
She turns green
to begin. The Natural History
peregrine, Peale's hawk
is forgetting to talk
like those coast homes
lost in the deeper part.

But to begin a procession
or a succession of lines
replacing the elms whose warps
and curves are called contradictions.

To begin, 'the stamp'
of autumn . . . these parades
whose curved names
folded in as pilgrims.
You start to swim
through a little darkness
and see some trees.

In the New Spring this
snow is the cold
water running off
what it was. The moth
loves the rose but who
does the rose love. It
goes and
around her
dusting some lady's clothes
from an edge like

trees, turning pages, around or
else about her, the wings marked
by eyes, and seeing twice.

SPEECH (ACROSS TIME)
"If, instead of whispering . . ."

The tract of voice
now in wave form.
Relative energy, decibels
a woman's rising
pitch clearly graphed.
"A stream of sound"
or jags of a large crowd
laughing. Spectrum
of harmonics; sound
pulls on sequent sound
as 'my name'. Sing
'a' [a] as in 'far'.

Holy Tuesday
bright with haze,
the Duke came.
Six oz. of bread.

Saturday:
San Piero.

Tuesday (Kalends):
the dry wind,
dinner with B—.

Thursday:
alone, the snow
not melting.
Twelve oz. at noon.

Friday:
head of the old man,
the raised arm,
dinner alone.

Monday:
legs of the lower figure,
the last of it.

Thursday 13TH
(Corpus Domini):
the blue field,
dinner with B—.

Monday: colder,
the child's torso.
Moon through the first quarter.

A VIEW OF MIAPLACIDUS

her invisible light and island
cities her parks
through the fire
rings and dark eyes
a star's woods and lakes.
Mid-December of our year
nearing solstice
a view of Miaplacidus
at a third remove.

A CURIOUS THING THE

houses are red and green
the ducks have gone while there's
room
and the ice is clear
on what is there when
to my eyes her mounting
losses over the years
the lines lately, turning corners.
It can be answered
"everything," like Pegasus
whose stars; in October
the Centaur opposite the sun.
As these figures, the weather
this winter rides over
is one thing, her
tears hanging down is
another, like trees or water
forms the edge of.
The curled lip always wet,
efforts ill-conceived,
"unlovely." Everything's
fat and unlovely
by the door. The
houses of red and green
of the various schemes.

AMONG VARIOUS

Among various
things to be signed.
Can you still mark each

interval by stars.
Two
colors mix in the pipe

one hiding l's and r's
and then the lost letters.
The table and

chairs, the bed
and my dead friend's
gift walk on regular feet.

In the morning his head
peels back and
hangs from its neck.

A hinged cut of
about six inches
scored with lines. The eyes

fix on bathroom windows
and women's clothes. Later
that night

she uses a different voice
to tell the future after
it arrives

without surprises. In general
more sleep. Think of it
as a science.

Watercolors and Drawings
Kandinsky Miro Calder
A room with five sides
for three years
A comb in the mirror
Her Longer Works
Paintings and Others

A REASONED REPLY TO GILBERT RYLE
(after Blake's Newton)

Sound becomes difficult
to dispose of

etc.. You go to sit down
and hope for a chair.

One of a pair of
eyes

distends.
Redness begins

on the left side.
The car always starts

in the morning
and it takes me

where someone else
is supposed to be

going
twice each week.

Or else the problem
of light and air.

Upstairs a small leak.
Trouble through the other

eye
which stays open

unless the window itself
is broken.

Green. "Leaved" to begin.
Leaved, a borrowed skin
like a stem
but shucked each year
how well does it hear
me
at all, quiet
near the city, to survive
now it has to be quiet.
And if I had a daughter
I'd give her over
or my son, to learn
different terms where
they travel
by dark, without sound
that close to underground.

FOR L.Z.

A reasonable ear
in music, Bottom,
let's have it
out of tongs
and bones, was it
tongues? "To gather"
or "to ring";
and damp bones
below the stone
arches, a man's jaw
displayed on dark paper
as the bridge came down
following the song.

A small poem about hawthorn
in spring white mays
and later full haws
MacDiarmid calls color
of heart's blood
over bright lobes
like certain eyes
excluding these
crystals of morphine
a stiff morris performed
for a tour, six
dancers rehearsing turns.

This cat and
my lady
are unkind to me
asleep when
I'm awake
then speaking
by the bed.

Allen says we let in no light
here, the windows face walls
the floors and walls covered with books
and we don't dance enough
which is true, make love enough
not true and write difficult poems
which is also true at times.
This time it isn't true
as anyone listening or
reading will notice.
There are friends here
sitting or standing and others
who are not friends. It's Friday
evening and we've been talking
about cities such as Boston and San Francisco
London's parks when it's clear
towns like Bremen still marked by war
and the red dirt of the Sierra Nevada
the signs everywhere "Mas Agua"
and the music you can't hear outside of Spain.
The talk is loud and everyone's laughing.
One reason is that Kit got back last night
still alive and has already begun
a new moustache, now legal.

sweet showers last
soft grey, light,
winter's passed

Figure
the gammadion
formed of four capital
gammas
in a cross
or voided Greek cross
the same gammadion
the gamma she reads
meaning cornerstone.

Once in October
not seeing
the Gegenschein
or counterglow
an elliptical light
opposite the sun
and near the ecliptic
in Sagittarius the centaur
'diurnal archer'.

You were right I
should have stayed. The snow
came down and
snow
the trees. My train
got in at three.

HAR'RI·ER (2,1)

any hawk
the genus of

grey hawk
spindle legged

feeds on tender animals
one who harries

(from *Harry*)
and insects through air

These are my glasses
I don't wear
This is the comb
for her hair

A VITRUVIAN FIGURE BY JUAN GRIS

begins with a line from Donne
or anyone, that drawes Natures workes
from Natures law
moving from the eyes and spare
features this time a woman's figure
defining a circle compressed
where the arms are too weak to extend.

Each day some features change.
The mirror with its own columns
and rosettes at each corner
has a yellow frame
where the Crucian beads are hanging,
but her own body in the diagram
tells two different times

that are constant
like the dots and irregular
curves the oval encloses
the way Gris painted it
at twenty-nine, supposedly
building up forms from
the separate parts, from the eyes
and empty features to the rounded
shoulders, the curve at the saddle
of bony hips, and the legs
spread wide marking
the limits of the ring.

A MEASURE

After waking he
waited.

In his mind were
three women.

Some eyes are red but dead men
have nothing to say
though they sit up and
talk to you
and their faces turn blue.

♉

The bull is
constant
wedded
to economy.

The bull is
steady.

A RING

SEVEN POEMS

A RING

Do you remember
when I broke that mirror that
time
so that in time
with lighted faces, talking.

Each in her place
as I remember it.

But the words they were
speaking.
I couldn't hear them
caught up as I was
in listening.

One part held an eye
another a raised arm
and she called to her brother
through them.

                    What was left
of the ring
became a question. Where
had they been all that time.

Or lost sight of
where had they gone.

A rabbit standing there
had the answer.
But he ran so much faster
he got lost in laughter.

And reading in this room
it was the same.
Now the man in the moon
has a name.

The boat cuts a lost
line straight across
40 to 56 across
Kansas and

across Kansas all
the machines of the water
the leaves were called decisions
resisted in photographs.

Of the earlier towers, clear rind
and horizon; some seven counted
shades of green or blue
finally grey.

   Each day
the open faces in threes
say it's easier
(unicorn phoenix Julius Caesar).

I got up at nine
and the leaves were

brown. What time
is it tonight.

I got down at three
and they were green

what do you mean
'do you want bacon.'

But that was later
with a mashed potato.

Who turned out the light
and turned it on.
Where is the book
he came from.

Which one. Here is a book
three days long
shaped like a tree
give it to me.

Here is a room
with a broken door.
It lasted a year
the time before.

Here is a finger
turning and turning.
It turned so long
it became a wall.

Actual memories mostly
the length of an arm;

a social art, things known
written down. This desk

deflects light
to my eyes, tests distance.

A toad in the garden now
dug out from winter's rest

interests cats.
Turning

through a finger
the elm's walls

are ideas, old leaves
apologise. Increasingly

the road
rises toward us

knowing and
womanly, leaning

from a window.

This is a room.

Give me this and
this. This

book ends some
time when it ends and

this is a room.

AN ALPHABET

When it rains each day the sky
turns grey and the water

flows down through the holes
onto the white walls

and wood floors
and over the clothes

and books and the comb
and the curve in the mirror.

And it falls on the woman
sleeping there

with her face hidden and her hair
across both pillows.

And the five-pointed leaves
are yellow and green.

Listen to me, she said,
listen to me.

They walk along and
talk to themselves

and the shoes and
windows and

listen to me
they get back in the tree.

THE OLD MOVIE
(Or Le Fou, June 1967)

I'm in it and it's
dark

and I'm reading Kit Smart.
Last night I lost my

watch (my clock),
but I'm coming out to

get it
and get you too.

So don't do anything
I wouldn't do.

HERE

I'm
here
to
give
this
reading
under
the
grey this
green
ceiling.

It
has
been
like
spring
here.
The
weather
veering

and
you
will
see
that
I
am
living
in
the
shadow
of
that
bridge.
It
is
so
quiet
here;

ITEM
a maistre Francoys Villon . . .

Item: come Robin Turgis to me
I'll pay him his wine
and his wife as well

    a great diviner
    if he finds me

and if my talk's foreign
I was taught by two women

    The one was young
    she danced and sang
    and moved to music
    and now she's gone

    The other you know
    is quiet and sad
    as hard as fair
    but not so bad

    She lives alone
    and lives with me
    and that's the way
    it will always be

Item: come Robin Turgis to me
I'll pay him his wine
and his wife as well

    a great diviner
    if he finds me

PROSE 1

Today I woke up and it was the following
stage. I lost the color from one eye
and my way of hearing changed. In the
mirror nothing was the same. The
building next door was gone and things
grew there in its place. My sense of
smell returned for the worse. An old
man smelled like a telephone booth. A
hitch-hiking girl wore perfume. One of
the plants in the living-room died.
Another one left town. I changed my
name not to be recognised. I changed
it to John, or Wanda. A wand chair is
wicker. A wandering dune has moved.
It passes the fixed stars in an ancient
catalogue. It's gone too soon. Too
little to choose. To you it all seems
silly. But there once was a fiddler
called Wandering Willie.

PROSE 2

In the game Milford threw a pass to
his receiver. He had a game leg but
he played. He had a way with the
ballgame and was a perfect aim. He
threw the ball through the air and it
stayed there. It stayed where. It
stayed in the cheerleader's yellow
hair. It stayed in the 50,000 seat
stadium. It stayed in America, on
the air.

PROSE 3

What is the moon. What is the woman
that climbed over them. Who could have
thought a zone of sun would keep them
warm. Great harm. Who can remember
numbers when they're wrong.

PROSE 9

Prose 9 is about the space between the
i and the v in 5. A donut approxi-
mation of the full moon appears be-
hind the central part of The Great Forest.
The entire city of trees lies in ruins
but the bird doesn't know it. It's
green but seems to be a city rather than
trees or else the remains of either one.
The sky is more grey than blue in
1927 and the boardwalk has fallen
leaving a mountain.

PROSE 12

The sunlight was the same as the plant
life but longer and darker. It was
the darkness of a great forest the size
of a five-legged chair. The ferns had
always been there before the paintings
on the wall. They had been there before
the numbers and the ladders. There were
hanged men in bogs and on cards. The
rain came down inside and outside and
the people walk by with wet faces and
green thumbs.

PROSE 13
a war

The accident that was supposed to have
happened the night before took place
again the next day. The highways were
covered with snow and under the window
were the rest of the tracks going to
a motel. An opening talked reluctantly
about losses. One side of the musician
collided with his own body on the way
to the grave and died immediately. Later
he was heard to say that it wouldn't have
happened if he had stayed in his room.
It had come to him in a dream the following
week but he had believed it to be a
beautiful woman. Besides in the end he
was no longer afraid of lies. It was
the moon cooking like a fried egg, or
the drowned lady's necklace of water-drops.

SPEECH (AGAIN)

human voice? but maybe the comparison
does run in circles. A burst of breath
and so on, likes music

and then most of the time life
a river but another one not
this one
emptying cities. No one says
How do you do now. Did anyone
ever say oo oo oo oo. Yes.
Four equal pulses of breath.

A writer said Hedge-
crickets sing, but that would form lines
in Ogam, even lies
on stones. Besides
none of the dying
soldiers would have chosen it

though equally four gentle pulses
(unequal), then three,
off the eaves, the water again
into the water.

Excess of eye or
                        exercise
And treating of light
Suffers and produces
Looking back its effects
The imprecise dreams
Shaping of leaves
Some chairs set toward
Music
          simple laws
Say the number three where
How is she near
Knock on the door
Unless we're not here

how pretty you are
maybe
more
than you believe
maybe less
than you think
you are pretty
you are prettier
than they
but don't be sad
one day
when someone wakes me
secretly
in a different
dream

(Picabia "L'Abime de la Perfection")

THE COMPLAINTS

medium height carefully shaved
astonished grey eyes or
                resigned

flower in boutonnière
             it is not

a passport photograph
of Jules Laforgue
          but a gift
from Gustave Kahn

the dark tie British jacket
           bureaucrat overcoat
whatever necessaries . . .
              always . . .
under an arm

The rare portraits
in grey Berlin streets
or Paris
        not pretty but

for him . . . as a concession
pleasing to women
         and winter '82

Berlin
        "here the blue sky
        heavy air
waves of April
        the beautiful women
        think it's spring

I trapped a fish
with my naked hand
It was covered with fur
and hard to understand

There was no hook
to shake
or orange birthday cake
like we've all

had to partake of
at one time
or another
This was a fish

without a friend
that met its end
smiling at the dish
Fish with your

yellow sleeves and
rolled up magazine
and open belly
when your eyes

clouded over
you looked like some other
bird
of a different color

Cats moved into the room
They walk on old shoes

They talk specifically
about They talk about

rabbit and plant life
Cat-talk is a habit

of understanding
The lowest leaves carry

teeth marks
into watery graves

The waves wash over
their yellow faces

Their faces are grey
When the war first came

they return to shore

and wonder if it's Wednesday
or the day before

After six days it
cleared in time for night
We went to a film and
saw the man kill an Indian
There's no more pure air
anywhere in America
says the paper. I
believe her
when she speaks to me
She doesn't care
Her Jewish eyes are Greek
always telling lies
But on film they look green
coming out of trees
I believe her
and they're brown
I see her for a while
crossing Montana
to the other side of
town. There
the car starts again
through the first snow
at the edge of Pocatello

Notes

Its form: New Spring—Neue Frühling, of Heine.

"Holy Tuesday": from the diary of Jacopo da Pontormo.

"A view of Miaplacidus": Miaplacidus is a star recently "seen" for the first time by a satellite monitoring infra-red light emissions.

For L.Z.: The London Bridge is now someplace in Arizona where they are making a river to go under it.

Here (*2*) and *Here* (*3*): from letters by Hart Crane.

****

I have also drawn or distorted a number of phrases from books such as: Webster's Second; Colin Cherry, *On Human Communication;* Willard Van Orman Quine, *Word and Object, From a Logical Point of View* ("On what there is").

*Printed July 1972 in Santa Barbara for
the Black Sparrow Press by Noel Young. Design
by Barbara Martin. This edition is limited to
750 copies in paper wrappers; 175 hardcover
copies numbered & signed by the poet; & 26
lettered copies handbound in boards by Earle
Gray, each with an original drawing by Bobbie
Creeley, signed by the poet & artist.*

Michael Palmer was born in New York City in 1943. He was educated at Harvard University and now lives and works in San Francisco.

Photo: *Tom McGuane*

I think that Michael Palmer was delivered two blocks astray in 1943 because he was aborted at our address two months before. Now he has arrived I think a long way from the Rhinelander apartments in Greenwich Village with a poetry addressed to occupant to refund the Indians for the Manhatta sell.

ROBERT DUNCAN